The Secret Ingredient

Tasty Recipes with an Unusual Twist

Gloria Hander Lyons

Blue Sage Press

The Secret Ingredient
Tasty Recipes with an Unusual Twist

Inquires should be addressed to:
Blue Sage Press
48 Borondo Pines
La Marque, TX 77568
www.BlueSagePress.com

ISBN: 978-0-9802244-1-2

Library of Congress Control Number: 2008900706

First Edition: March, 2008

Printed in the United States of America

Table of Contents

Introduction
The Secret Ingredient: Tasty Recipes with an Unusual Twist

For years, proud cooks have boasted that their own special version of a popular recipe included a "secret ingredient" that made their dish exceptional. They carefully guarded this "top secret" information to maintain a culinary edge over their competition.

Out of sheer boredom, many cooks began combining common ingredients in dishes where you'd least expect to find them, in an attempt to spark their own creativity and surprise and delight the taste buds of their families and dinner guests.

Many other unusual ingredient combinations came about because of cooking contests sponsored by large food and beverage corporations in their quest to generate more sales for their products. Cooks everywhere challenged their culinary expertise to concoct thousands of tasty recipes that have been passed down from generation to generation. And the search for these unique flavor combinations continues to this day.

The Secret Ingredient: Tasty Recipes with an Unusual Twist is a collection of just a small sampling of these recipes for using familiar ingredients in an unexpected combination.

Some are tried and true favorites, developed many years ago, like Apple Pie with Ketchup, 7-Up Cherry Cobbler, Chocolate Mayonnaise Cake, Cola Sloppy Joe's and Popcorn Salad.

Others are delectable new concoctions like Pork n' Bean Bread, Chicken with Maple Syrup, Kool-Aid Barbecue Pork Ribs, Tomato Soup Crock Pot Cake and Twinkie Ice Cream Shake.

This cookbook includes more than 90 uncommonly delicious recipes for beverages, appetizers, soups, salads, breads, sauces, main dishes, side dishes, sandwiches and desserts that use common ingredients with an unusual twist. You'll want to try them all!

But while you're experimenting, don't forget to let your creativity run wild—you might just concoct a distinctively different recipe with your very own "secret ingredient".

The
Secret
Ingredient:

Beverages

Spiced Hot Tea

3/4 cup unsweetened instant tea powder
1 teaspoon finely grated orange peel
1 teaspoon ground cinnamon
1/2 teaspoon ground cloves
1/4 teaspoon ground nutmeg
1 (14 oz.) can sweetened condensed milk
6-1/3 cups water

Secret
Ingredient:
Condensed
Milk

In large saucepan, combine tea, orange peel and spices. Add water; mix well. Stir in sweetened condensed milk. Heat over medium heat until very hot, but do not boil.

Tropical Crock Pot Tea

6 cups boiling water
6 tea bags
1-1/2 cups pineapple juice
1-1/2 cups orange juice
1/3 cup granulated sugar
1 orange, thinly sliced (unpeeled)
2 tablespoons honey

Secret
Ingredient:
Pineapple
Juice

Turn crock pot on to LOW setting. Add boiling water and tea bags. Cover and let stand 5 minutes. Remove tea bags. Stir in remaining ingredients. Cover and heat on low for 2-3 hours. Serve tea from crock pot.

Sun Rise Iced Coffee

3 cups strong black coffee, chilled
1/2 cup orange juice
1-1/2 cups club soda

Secret Ingredient: Orange Juice

In a 1-1/2 quart pitcher, blend orange juice and coffee together. Gently stir in club soda. Pour into glasses filled with ice. Makes 6 servings.

Very Berry Iced Coffee

1 (10 oz.) package frozen blackberries
1/2 cup granulated sugar
1/2 cup water
9 cups chilled black coffee
1 pint half-and-half
1 cup sweetened whipped cream or frozen non-dairy
    whipped topping, thawed

Secret Ingredient: Black-Berries

Place frozen blackberries, sugar and water in a blender and puree. Strain mixture into a large pitcher. Add the coffee and half-and-half. Blend well. Pour into 12-ounce glasses partially filled with crushed ice. Top with whipped cream. Makes 10-12 servings.

Banana Smoothie

2 large ripe bananas, sliced & frozen
2 cups milk
1/4 cup creamy peanut butter
2 tablespoons granulated sugar

Secret
Ingredient:
Peanut
Butter

Place all ingredients in a blender or food processor. Blend until smooth. Pour into 2 tall glasses and serve immediately.

Tea-Time Ice Cream Soda

1-1/2 cups boiling water
6 tea bags
1/4 cup granulated sugar
3 cups apple juice, chilled
3 cups ginger ale, chilled
Vanilla ice cream

Secret
Ingredient:
Apple
Juice

Steep tea bags in boiling water for 5 minutes. Remove tea bags. Stir in sugar. Let mixture cool. In a large pitcher, combine tea and juice. Just before serving, stir in ginger ale. Pour into glasses and top with 1 scoop of ice cream. Makes 8 servings.

New England Coffee Latte

3 cups strong black coffee
2 cups half-and-half
1 cup maple syrup
Sweetened whipped cream (optional)
Ground cinnamon (optional)

Secret
Ingredient:
Maple
Syrup

Heat half-and-half and maple syrup in a saucepan over medium heat until very hot. Do not boil. Stir in the coffee. Pour into cups. Top with whipped cream and sprinkle lightly with cinnamon if desired. Makes 6 servings.

Magic Potion Chocolate Punch

1/2 cup chocolate-flavored syrup
2 cups milk
2 (12 oz.) cans cola beverage,
    room temperature
Non-dairy whipped topping, if desired

Secret
Ingredient:
Cola

In a 4-cup microwaveable measuring cup, blend chocolate syrup and milk. Microwave on high power 3-4 minutes or until hot. Divide chocolate milk into 8 mugs. Slowly pour about 1/3 cup of cola into each mug. Top with whipped topping.

Party-Time Ice Cream Shake

2-1/2 cups milk
6 Hostess® Twinkie singles
1/2 cup chocolate syrup (optional)
3 cups vanilla ice cream

Secret
Ingredient:
Twinkies

In a food processor, blend milk, Twinkies and chocolate syrup 5 to 10 seconds. Add ice cream and blend until smooth. Pour into glasses. Makes 6 servings.

Strawberry Cheesecake Punch

2 (10 oz.) packages frozen sweetened
  strawberries, thawed
1 (8 oz.) pkg. cream cheese, softened
1/2 cup cream of coconut
2 cups milk
1 quart vanilla ice cream

Secret
Ingredient:
Cream
Cheese

In a blender, combine strawberries, cream cheese, and cream of coconut. Blend until smooth. Pour into a punch bowl. Stir in milk. Drop small scoops of ice cream into punch. Recipe makes about 16 servings.

The
Secret
Ingredient:

Breads &
Breakfast
Foods

Light 'n Nutty Pancakes

1-1/4 cups all-purpose flour
2 tablespoons sugar
2 teaspoons baking powder
1/2 teaspoon salt
1-1/4 cups milk
1 large egg
1/4 cup peanut butter

Secret
Ingredient:
Peanut
Butter

Combine flour, sugar, baking powder and salt. Beat milk with egg and peanut butter until smooth. Add to dry ingredients and stir just until moistened. Lightly butter hot griddle. Use a 1/4 cup measure to pour batter for each pancake onto griddle. Cook until bubbles form on top of batter. Turn over and cook until golden brown on remaining side.

Nutty Maple Syrup

1 cup maple syrup
1/2 cup peanut butter

Secret
Ingredient:
Peanut
Butter

Combine syrup and peanut butter in a small sauce pan. Cook over medium heat, stirring until smooth and heated through. Serve over pancakes.

High-Rise Pancakes

1-1/4 cups sifted flour
2 teaspoons baking powder
1 tablespoon sugar
1/2 teaspoon salt
1 large egg, slightly beaten
1/4 cup milk
3/4 cup 7-UP (room temperature)
2 tablespoons melted butter or margarine

Secret
Ingredient:
7-Up

In a large bowl, blend flour, baking powder, sugar and salt. In a small bowl, combine egg, milk, and butter; add to dry ingredients, stirring just until moistened. Batter will be slightly lumpy. Lightly grease hot griddle. Use a 1/4 cup measure to pour batter for each pancake onto griddle. Cook until bubbles form on top of batter. Turn over and cook until golden brown on remaining side. Makes about 8 pancakes.

Mayan Maple Syrup

1-1/2 cups maple syrup
1/2 stick (1/4 cup) butter
3 tablespoons unsweetened cocoa powder
Dash of salt

Secret
Ingredient:
Chocolate

In a small sauce pan heat maple syrup and butter over medium heat until butter is melted. Add cocoa powder and salt, stirring until well blended. Serve warm over ice cream, pound cake, pancakes or waffles. Store in an airtight container in the refrigerator for up to 1 week.

Orange Breakfast Muffins

1-1/2 cups cornflakes
2 cups all-purpose flour
1 tablespoon baking powder
1/2 teaspoon salt
1/2 cup butter or margarine, softened
1/2 cup granulated sugar
2 large eggs
1 tablespoon grated orange zest
1 cup orange juice
1/2 cup raisins
1/2 cup chopped nuts

Secret
Ingredient:
Corn
Flakes

Preheat oven to 350°. Crush cornflakes to measure 3/4 cup; set aside. In a small bowl, blend flour, baking powder and salt. In a large bowl, cream together butter and sugar until fluffy. Add eggs and orange zest; beat again. Stir in orange juice. Add flour mixture, stirring until just moistened. Stir in cornflakes, raisins and nuts. Fill greased muffin tins 3/4 full. Bake for 20-25 minutes or until done. Cool 10 minutes before removing from pan. Makes about 12 muffins.

Cheesy Sausage Muffins

1 lb. bulk pork sausage
1 can condensed cheese soup
1-1/2 soup cans of water
3 cups biscuit mix

Secret
Ingredient:
Cheese
Soup

Preheat oven to 350°. Grease 24 muffin cups. In a medium skillet, cook sausage; drain. In a large bowl, mix soup and water. Stir in sausage and biscuit mix. Fill muffin cups about half full. Bake 15-20 minutes or until golden brown.

Bean Town Bread

2 cups sugar
1 cup vegetable oil
3 eggs
1 (16 oz.) can pork-n-beans, drained
2 cups flour
1 teaspoon ground cinnamon
1/2 teaspoon baking soda
1/2 teaspoon baking powder
1 teaspoon vanilla extract
1 cup chopped nuts
1 cup raisins

Secret
Ingredient:
Pork 'n
Beans

Preheat oven to 325°.

In a mixing bowl, beat sugar, oil, eggs and beans with electric mixer until mixture is smooth. Stir in flour, cinnamon, soda and baking powder until combined. Stir in vanilla, raisins and nuts.

Pour into two greased and floured 8 x 4" loaf pans. Bake 50 to 55 minutes or until done. Cool in pans 5 minutes. Remove and cool on wire racks.

Spring Garden Bread

1 cup peeled, grated cucumber (about 1 large)
1 cup granulated sugar
1/2 cup vegetable oil
1 teaspoon vanilla extract
2 large eggs
1-1/2 cups all-purpose flour
1 teaspoon ground cinnamon
1/2 teaspoon salt
1/2 teaspoon baking soda
1/4 teaspoon baking powder
1/2 cup chopped pecans

Secret Ingredient: Cucumber

Preheat oven to 350°.

In a large mixing bowl, combine cucumber, sugar, oil, vanilla extract and eggs. Beat until well blended. In a separate bowl, mix flour, cinnamon, salt, baking powder and baking soda. Stir into the cucumber mixture. Add pecans. Pour into a 9 x 5" greased and floured loaf pan. Bake 55-60 minutes or until done. Remove from pan and cool on wire rack.

Tangy Herb Biscuits

2 cups self-rising flour
1/4 cup mayonnaise
1 teaspoon dried sage leaves, crumbled
1 teaspoon dried thyme
1 cup milk

Secret
Ingredient:
Mayonnaise

Preheat oven to 400°. Grease a 12-cup muffin pan with vegetable oil. In a large bowl, stir together flour, mayonnaise, sage, thyme and milk just until moistened. Do not over mix. Divide batter evenly into muffin cups. Bake for 12 to 15 minutes or until golden brown.

Mediterranean Cornbread

1 (6 oz.) pkg. cornbread mix
1/4 teaspoon garlic powder
1/8 teaspoon ground red pepper (optional)
2/3 cup milk
1 large egg, slightly beaten
1/2 cup shredded Cheddar cheese
1/2 cup sliced pimiento-stuffed green olives

Secret
Ingredient:
Olives

Preheat oven to 375°. In a medium bowl, combine cornbread mix, garlic powder and pepper. In a small bowl, combine milk and egg. Stir egg mixture into cornbread mix just until moistened. Add cheese and olives; stirring until blended. Pour batter into a greased 8 x 4" loaf pan. Bake 25-30 minutes or until done. Cool in pan 5 before removing. Serve warm.

New Year's Day Cornbread

1 lb. bulk pork sausage
1/2 cup chopped onion
1 cup cornmeal
1/2 cup flour
1 teaspoon salt
1/2 teaspoon baking soda
1 cup buttermilk
2 large eggs, slightly beaten
1/2 cup vegetable oil
1 (4 oz.) can chopped green chilies, drained
2 cups grated cheddar cheese
3/4 cup cream style corn
1 (15 oz.) can black-eyed peas, drained

Secret Ingredient: Black-Eyed Peas

Preheat oven to 350°.

Brown sausage and onion in a skillet; drain and set aside. In a large bowl, combine cornmeal, flour, salt and baking soda. In a separate bowl, mix together eggs, buttermilk and oil. Stir egg mixture into cornmeal mixture just until moistened. Add cooked sausage and onion, green chilies, corn, cheese and peas; blend well.

Pour into greased 9 x 13" baking pan. Bake 40 to 45 min. or until golden brown and toothpick inserted in center comes out clean. Cut into squares and serve warm.

The Secret Ingredient:

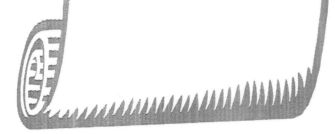

Appetizers

"Which Came First" Deviled Eggs

6 hard-boiled eggs
1/2 cup finely chopped cooked chicken
3 tablespoons mayonnaise
1 tablespoon dill pickle relish
2 teaspoons grated onion
1 teaspoon prepared mustard
1 teaspoon dried parsley flakes
Salt & pepper to taste
Paprika, for garnish

Secret Ingredient: Chicken

Cut eggs lengthwise in half. Place yolks in a bowl and mash with a fork. Add chicken, mayonnaise, relish, onion, mustard, parsley, salt and pepper. Mix until well blended. Fill egg whites with egg yolk mixture. Sprinkle lightly with paprika. Cover and refrigerate until ready to serve.

Celebration Cheese Spread

1 pound Cheddar cheese, cut into chunks
4 ounces cream cheese, softened
1/2 cup Champagne
1 teaspoon dried parsley flakes
1/2 teaspoon ground nutmeg
1/8 teaspoon ground red pepper

Secret Ingredient: Champagne

Place all ingredients in bowl of food processor and process until smooth. Spoon mixture into a serving bowl. Cover and refrigerate at least 2 hours or until ready to serve. Let stand at room temperature for about 15 minutes to soften slightly. Serve with cut-up vegetables, crackers or French bread slices.

Saucy Meatballs

1 (16 oz.) bag frozen, cooked meatballs
1 (12 oz.) jar grape jelly
1 cup barbecue sauce

Secret
Ingredient:
Grape
Jelly

In a large saucepan, combine jelly and barbecue sauce. Cook over medium heat until jelly melts. Add meatballs. Heat over medium-low heat, stirring occasionally, for about 15 minutes, or until meatballs are hot. Serve on a platter or in a crock pot set on LOW.

Tipsy Chicken Wings

50 chicken wings (wing tips removed)
2 (12-ounce) bottles of beer
1 cup molasses
1/2 cup creamy peanut butter
1/2 cup lemon juice
1/2 cup Worcestershire sauce
1/4 cup prepared mustard
1 teaspoon salt
2 tablespoons chili powder

Secret
Ingredients:
Beer &
Peanut
Butter

Preheat oven to 450°. Line a large baking pan with foil. Cut chicken wings in half at the joint and place in baking pan. In a large saucepan, combine remaining ingredients. Bring to a boil and cook over low heat about 15 minutes until sauce has reduced and thickened. Pour sauce over wings, tossing to coat. Bake for 20 minutes, or until done. Remove from oven and let rest for 10 minutes. Serve warm.

Cheese Dip Surprise

1 (16 oz.) package Velveeta cheese,
    cut into cubes
1 cup chopped apples, unpeeled
1 tablespoon brown sugar
1/4 teaspoon ground cinnamon
1/2 cup sour cream

Secret
Ingredient:
Apples

In a large, microwave-safe bowl, mix together cheese, apples, brown sugar and cinnamon. Microwave on high power 4 to 5 minutes or until cheese is completely melted, stirring halfway through cooking time. Stir in sour cream. Serve warm with crackers.

Hot & Spicy Chocolate Dip

1 cup semisweet chocolate chips
2 tablespoons butter or margarine
1/3 cup granulated sugar
1 teaspoon hot pepper sauce
1/3 cup water

Secret
Ingredient:
Hot Pepper
Sauce

Combine chocolate chips, sugar, water and butter in small saucepan. Cook over medium heat, stirring constantly until chocolate chips are melted. Do not boil. Remove from heat and stir in hot pepper sauce. Serve warm with pieces of pound cake or fruit for dipping.

Fruity Avocado Dip

2 avocados, peeled & chopped
1/2 cup raisins
1/2 cup vegetable oil
1/4 cup lime juice
1 teaspoon granulated sugar
1 teaspoon salt
1/4 teaspoon ground black pepper

Secret
Ingredient:
Raisins

Place all ingredients in a blender or food processor. Cover and process on high speed until smooth, about 45 seconds. Serve with raw vegetables, crackers or tortilla chips. Makes about 1-2/3 cups.

Doctored-Up Bean Dip

1 (15 oz.) can red kidney beans,
   drained & mashed
3 tablespoons tomato paste
2 tablespoons vegetable oil
1/2 teaspoon salt
1/4 teaspoon ground black pepper
1/4 teaspoon garlic powder
1/2 cup Dr. Pepper™
1 (4 oz.) can chopped green chilies, drained
1 teaspoon Worcestershire sauce
1 cup shredded Cheddar cheese
4 slices bacon, cooked and crumbled

Secret
Ingredient:
Dr. Pepper

In a medium saucepan, combine all ingredients. Heat over medium-high heat until cheese is melted. Serve warm with tortilla chips.

Sweet & Spicy Chips & Salsa

Tortillas:
4 flour tortillas
2 tablespoons butter or margarine, melted
2 tablespoons granulated sugar
3/4 teaspoon ground cinnamon

Secret
Ingredient:
Strawberries

Salsa:
2 cups strawberries, chopped
1 tablespoon fresh mint, chopped
1 tablespoon lime juice
1/2 teaspoon grated lime zest
1-1/2 teaspoons honey

To prepare salsa: Combine strawberries, mint, lime juice, lime zest and honey in a medium bowl. Cover and refrigerate for at least one hour.

To prepare tortillas: Preheat oven to 375°. Brush both sides of each tortilla with butter. Combine sugar and cinnamon in a small bowl. Sprinkle over both sides of each tortilla.

Bake tortillas on lightly greased baking sheet for about 10 minutes or until crisp and golden. Cut into quarters. Serve with salsa.

The Secret Ingredient:

Salads

Frozen Banana Salad

1 cup granulated sugar
1 cup buttermilk
2 medium bananas, mashed
1 cup pecans, chopped
1 (8 oz.) container frozen non-dairy
    whipped topping, thawed

Secret
Ingredient:
Butter-
Milk

In a large bowl, blend sugar with buttermilk. Stir in mashed bananas and pecans. Gently fold in whipped topping. Pour into a shallow baking pan and freeze until firm. Remove from freezer about 15 minutes before serving. Cut into squares to serve.

Cherry Gelatin Salad

1 (16 oz.) can pitted Bing cherries
1 (20 oz.) can crushed pineapple
1 (3 oz.) pkg. black cherry gelatin
1 (3 oz.) pkg. red raspberry gelatin
1 (8 oz.) pkg. cream cheese, softened
1-1/2 cups cola beverage
1 cup chopped pecans

Secret
Ingredient:
Cola

Drain juice from cherries and pineapple into a 2 cup measuring cup and add enough water to make 1-1/2 cups. Pour into a medium saucepan and bring to a boil. Place gelatin in a large bowl and stir in hot juice mixture. Add the cream cheese and stir until cheese is melted. Let cool. Stir in cherries, pineapple, nuts and cola. Pour into a shallow casserole dish, cover and chill several hours until set.

Creamy Tropical Chicken Salad

2-1/2 cups diced cooked chicken
1-1/2 cups pineapple chunks or tidbits
1/2 cup chopped walnuts or pecans
1 cup frozen non-dairy whipped
    topping, thawed
3/4 cup mayonnaise

Secret
Ingredient:
Whipped
Topping

In a large bowl, mix chicken, pineapple and nuts. In a small bowl, blend together whipped topping and mayonnaise. Gently stir into chicken mixture. Cover and refrigerate for several hours. Serve on top of lettuce leaves arranged on a plate. Top with a maraschino cherry if desired. Makes 5-6 servings.

Country Kitchen Salad

3 cups crumbled cornbread
1/2 lb. bacon, cooked and crumbled
    (8-10 slices)
1 cup shredded Cheddar cheese
1/2 cup chopped green pepper
1/4 cup chopped green onion
1 large tomato, chopped
1 (8 oz.) can whole kernel corn, drained
1/2 cup mayonnaise
Salt & pepper to taste

Secret
Ingredient:
Cornbread

Mix all ingredients together in a large bowl. Cover and chill for several hours to blend flavors. Makes 6-8 servings.

Cheesy Corn Salad

1/2 cup chopped green onion
1 cup chopped celery
1/2 cup water chestnuts, chopped
3/4 cup mayonnaise
3/4 cup cooked and crumbled bacon
    (6-8 slices)
1 cup shredded Cheddar cheese
6 cups popped popcorn

Secret
Ingredient:
Popcorn

In a medium bowl, combine onion, celery, water chestnuts and mayonnaise. Cover and refrigerate until ready to serve. Just before serving stir in bacon, cheese and popcorn until well blended.

Garden Tuna Salad

1 (6 oz.) can solid white albacore tuna,
    drained
1 cup shredded carrots
1 cup celery, finely chopped
1 tablespoon grated onion
1/2 cup mayonnaise
1 cup canned shoestring potatoes

Secret
Ingredient:
Shoestring
Potatoes

In a medium bowl, combine all ingredients except potatoes. Cover and refrigerate until ready to serve. Just before serving stir in potatoes.

Crunchy Pinto Bean Salad

2 (15 oz.) cans pinto beans, drained
1 cup chopped green pepper
1 cup chopped onion
1 cup chopped tomato
5-6 cups chopped lettuce
1 cup shredded Cheddar cheese
1 (9-3/4 oz.) bag corn chips
1 (8 oz.) bottle Catalina dressing or to taste

Secret Ingredient: Corn Chips

In a large bowl, blend together first 4 ingredients. Cover and chill until ready to serve. Just before serving, add lettuce, cheese, corn chips and salad dressing and toss to coat. Makes about 8-10 servings.

Cool Summer Salad

4 cups watermelon chunks or balls, chilled
1/2 cup cream cheese, softened
2 tablespoons mayonnaise
1/2 cup whipping cream
2 tablespoons granulated sugar
1-1/4 cups finely chopped celery
1/4 cup finely chopped red bell pepper
1/2 cup chopped pecans

Secret Ingredient: Watermelon

Blend cream cheese with mayonnaise. Whip cream with sugar until soft peaks form. Fold into cream cheese mixture. Gently stir in celery and bell pepper. Place watermelon balls in 8 dessert glasses and spoon dressing over top. Sprinkle with pecans.

Pork Tenderloin Salad

1 whole pork tenderloin
1 (10 oz.) jar peach preserves
1/4 cup white wine vinegar
2 tablespoons Dijon mustard
1 (10 oz.) pkg. mixed salad greens
2 cups fresh or frozen (thawed) peach
    slices or 1 (16 oz.) can sliced peaches, drained
1 cup fresh or frozen raspberries, thawed
1 small red onion, cut into 1/8" thick slices
    and separated into rings
1/2 cup alfalfa sprouts

Secret Ingredient: Peaches

In a small bowl, blend preserves, vinegar and mustard. Remove about 1/2 cup of mixture for basting meat.

Cut pork tenderloin in half lengthwise, cutting to but not through bottom; open and flatten. Brush with about 1/3 cup of preserve mixture removed for basting. Place on broiling pan; broil 4 to 6 inches from heat 5 to 6 minutes. Turn; brush with another 2 tablespoons of basting mixture. Broil about 7 minutes or until done.

Arrange greens on four plates. Cut pork tenderloin into 1/2-inch thick slices. Place pork slices, peaches, raspberries, onion rings and alfalfa sprouts on greens. Drizzle with preserve mixture.

The
Secret
Ingredient:

Soups
& Stews

Georgia Planter's Soup

1/2 cup celery, finely chopped
1/4 cup onion, finely chopped
2 tablespoons butter or margarine
2 tablespoons all-purpose flour
2 cups chicken broth
2 cups milk
3/4 cup creamy peanut butter
Salt & pepper to taste
Chopped roasted peanuts for garnish, optional

Secret
Ingredient:
Peanut
Butter

Sauté onion and celery in butter until tender. Add flour, stirring until smooth and cook for 1 minute. Gradually add broth; bring mixture to a boil and stir until thickened. Stir in peanut butter. Add milk and stir until well blended. Simmer 10 minutes, stirring frequently. Season with salt and pepper to taste. Garnish each serving with chopped peanuts if desired. Makes about 5 cups of soup.

Southern Belle Blush

2 (16 oz.) cans sliced peaches, drained
1 (8-oz.) container sour cream
1 cup pineapple juice
1/2 cup orange juice
2 tablespoons sugar

Secret
Ingredient:
Peaches

Process peaches in blender until smooth. Add remaining ingredients and process until well blended. Pour into bowl, cover and chill until ready to serve. Makes about 5-1/2 cups.

Greek Chicken Soup

6 cups chicken broth
1 teaspoon instant chicken
   bouillon granules
1/2 cup uncooked regular rice
1/2 cup diced carrots
1/2 cup chopped celery
1/4 cup chopped onion
2-1/2 cups chopped, cooked chicken
2 tablespoons butter or margarine
2 tablespoons all-purpose flour
2 large eggs
1/4 cup lemon juice
Salt & pepper to taste

Secret Ingredients: Lemon & Eggs

In a large saucepan, combine chicken broth, bouillon, rice, carrots, celery and onion. Bring to a boil. Cover and simmer 20 minutes or until rice and vegetables are tender. Stir in chicken. Remove soup mixture from heat.

In a small saucepan, melt butter. Stir in flour. Cook 1 minute, stirring constantly until smooth. Gradually stir in 2 cups of broth from soup mixture. Cook, stirring constantly, until thickened. Remove from heat.

In a small bowl, beat eggs until frothy. Gradually stir in lemon juice and the 2 cups of thickened broth mixture. Slowly add egg mixture to soup mixture, stirring constantly. Heat gently until soup thickens slightly, stirring frequently. Do not boil or eggs will curdle. Add salt and pepper to taste. Makes about 4-5 servings.

Real Man's Chili

2 lbs. ground sirloin
1/2 cup chopped onion
1 (8 oz.) can tomato sauce
1 (16 oz.) can pinto beans, drained
1 (14 oz.) can diced tomatoes
1 cup beer
2 teaspoons instant beef bouillon granules
1 teaspoon unsweetened cocoa powder
1 teaspoon chili powder
1/2 teaspoon garlic powder
1/2 teaspoon dried oregano
1/4 teaspoon cayenne pepper (or to taste)
Salt to taste

Secret Ingredients: Beer & Chocolate

In a Dutch oven, cook ground beef and onions until beef is no longer pink; drain. Add remaining ingredients. Simmer uncovered for about 30 minutes, stirring occasionally. Makes about 6 servings.

Chilled Honeydew Soup

3-1/2 cups cubed honeydew melon
1/2 cup frozen limeade concentrate,
     thawed
1 cup dry sparkling white wine or
     Champagne

Secret Ingredient: Champagne

Place melon and limeade in blender or food processor; puree. Transfer to a large mixing bowl. Stir in sparkling wine. Cover. Chill for at least 2 hours. Pour into chilled soup bowls to serve. Makes 4-6 servings.

Santa Fe Tortilla Soup

2-1/2 cups chicken broth
1 cup heavy cream
1 (15 oz.) can pumpkin puree
2 tablespoons brown sugar, packed
1/2 teaspoon ground cumin
1/2 teaspoon chili powder
1/8 teaspoon ground nutmeg
3/4 cup grated cheddar cheese
Tortilla chips, coarsely crushed

Secret
Ingredient:
Pumpkin

Combine first 7 ingredients in a large saucepan and bring to a boil. Reduce heat and simmer about 15 minutes, stirring frequently, until soup thickens slightly. Season with salt and pepper to taste. Ladle soup into bowls and top with cheese and tortilla chips.

Ranch Hand Beef Soup

1 pound ground sirloin
1/2 cup chopped onion
1 (15 oz.) can white hominy, drained
1 (15 oz.) can pinto beans, drained
1 (14 oz.) can diced tomatoes
2 cups water
1 (1 oz.) envelope Ranch Dressing mix
2 teaspoons instant beef bouillon granules
1 teaspoon chili powder
1/2 teaspoon ground cumin

Secret
Ingredient:
Ranch
Dressing
Mix

In a Dutch oven, brown meat and onion together. Drain. Stir in remaining ingredients. Bring to a boil. Simmer for about 15 minutes, stirring occasionally. Add salt & pepper to taste. Top each serving with grated Cheddar cheese, sour cream and coarsely crushed tortilla chips.

Autumn Harvest Beef Stew

1-1/2 pounds lean beef stew meat
Salt and ground black pepper
1/4 cup all-purpose flour
2 tablespoons vegetable oil
1 cup apple juice (or apple cider)
1-1/2 cups water
1/2 cup chopped onion
1/2 cup sliced celery
2 teaspoons instant beef bouillon granules
1/4 teaspoon garlic powder
1 cup peeled and sliced carrots
2 cups peeled and diced potatoes
1/2 cup frozen green peas

Secret
Ingredient:
Apple
Juice

Season beef with salt and pepper and coat with flour. Heat oil in a Dutch oven. Add meat and brown on all sides. Stir in apple juice, water, onion, celery, beef bouillon and garlic powder; bring to a boil. Cover and simmer 30-40 minutes, stirring occasionally. Stir in carrots and potatoes. Cover and simmer another 30 minutes, stirring occasionally, until vegetables and meat are tender. Add peas, cover and cook for another 10 minutes.

The
Secret
Ingredient:

Main
Dishes

Crunchy Baked Chicken

6 boneless, skinless chicken breasts
1 medium size bag potato chips, crushed
1 stick butter or margarine
1/2 teaspoon salt
1/4 teaspoon pepper
1/4 teaspoon garlic powder
1/2 teaspoon onion powder
1/2 teaspoon paprika
1 teaspoon Worcestershire sauce

Secret
Ingredient:
Potato
Chips

Preheat oven to 350°. Grease a shallow baking dish. In a small, microwaveable bowl, melt butter in microwave. Stir in salt, pepper, garlic powder, onion powder, paprika and Worcestershire sauce. Dip chicken in butter mixture then roll in potato chips. Place chicken in prepared pan and bake 45 minutes or until done.

Chuck Wagon Roast Beef

1 (3-4 lb.) beef rump roast
1 can cream of mushroom soup
1 can cream of celery soup
1 small onion, chopped
1 cup milk
1 cup coffee

Secret
Ingredient:
Coffee

Place roast in a 4-1/2 quart crock pot. Sprinkle with salt and pepper. Combine remaining ingredients in a large bowl and blend well. Pour over roast and cook on LOW 8-10 hours or on HIGH 4-5 hours or until tender.

Tangy Pork Chops

8 (1/2" thick) pork chops
3/4 cup cola beverage
3/4 cup ketchup
1/4 teaspoon garlic powder
Salt & ground black pepper
1/4 cup brown sugar, packed

Secret
Ingredient:
Cola

Preheat oven to 350°. Place pork chops in a 9" x13" baking dish. In a small bowl, mix together cola, ketchup and garlic powder. Pour over chops. Sprinkle lightly with salt & pepper. Top with brown sugar. Bake uncovered for about 35 minutes, or until done.

Italian Spaghetti Bake

2 pounds ground sirloin
1 cup chopped onion
1 teaspoon dried basil leaves
1/2 teaspoon dried oregano
1/2 teaspoon garlic powder
1/2 teaspoon salt
1/4 teaspoon ground black pepper
1 (12 oz.) can Dr. Pepper™
2 (8 oz.) cans tomato sauce
1 tablespoon Worcestershire sauce
1 (16 oz.) package spaghetti, cooked & drained
1-1/2 cups shredded mozzarella cheese

Secret
Ingredient:
Dr. Pepper

Brown beef and onion in a Dutch oven over medium-high heat. Drain fat. Add seasonings, Dr. Pepper, tomato sauce and Worcestershire sauce. Bring to a boil and simmer for about 15-20 minutes, stirring occasionally. Stir in cooked spaghetti and cheese. Pour spaghetti mixture into a greased casserole dish. Bake at 350° for 20 minutes.

Chicken Mole

8 boneless skinless chicken breasts
1/4 cup olive oil
1 medium onion, chopped
1 clove garlic, minced
1 (4 oz.) can chopped green chilies,
    drained
1 (8 oz.) can tomato sauce
1 cup chicken broth
2 tablespoons granulated sugar
1 teaspoon chili powder
1 teaspoon salt
1/4 teaspoon ground black pepper
1 ounce unsweetened baking chocolate
2 tablespoons creamy peanut butter

Secret Ingredients: Chocolate & Peanut Butter

In a large skillet, brown the chicken breasts in olive oil. Remove chicken and set aside. In the same skillet, sauté onion and garlic over medium heat until tender. Stir in remaining ingredients. Cook over medium low heat until chocolate is melted. Add browned chicken, cover and simmer for about 30 minutes or until chicken is done, turning occasionally.

Easy Baked Salmon

4 salmon fillets (about 4 oz. each)
1/4 cup mayonnaise
Salt & ground black pepper

Secret
Ingredient:
Mayonnaise

Preheat oven to 400°. Arrange salmon on a lightly greased baking pan. Brush with mayonnaise. Sprinkle with salt and pepper. Bake 10 minutes or until fish flakes easily with a fork.

Barbecued Pork Ribs

1 cup barbecue sauce
3 tablespoons Kool-Aid Orange Flavor
   Sugar-Sweetened Soft Drink Mix
4 lbs. pork spareribs

Secret
Ingredient:
Kool-Aid

Preheat grill to medium-low heat. In a small bowl, mix barbecue sauce and drink mix until well blended. Place half of the ribs in a single layer in the center of a sheet of heavy-duty aluminum foil. Spoon half of sauce mixture over ribs. Bring up foil sides. Double fold top and ends to seal packet, leaving room for heat circulation inside. Repeat for remaining half of ribs.

Place packets on grate of grill; cover with lid. Grill for about 1-1/2 hours or until ribs are very tender. Remove from foil. Skim fat from sauce and serve with ribs.

Baked Almond Chicken

1 (2-1/2 to 3 lb.) chicken, cut into pieces
Salt and pepper to taste
1/2 cup maple syrup
1/4 cup butter or margarine, melted
2 teaspoons lemon juice
1/2 teaspoon grated lemon zest
1/4 cup sliced almonds

Secret
Ingredient:
Maple
Syrup

Preheat oven to 350°. Place chicken pieces in a shallow buttered baking dish. In a small bowl, blend syrup, butter, lemon juice and lemon zest. Pour over chicken. Sprinkle with salt and pepper. Sprinkle almonds over chicken. Bake uncovered 45 minutes or until done, basting occasionally.

Sunset Glazed Fish Filets

2 lbs. fish fillets
1 clove garlic, minced
2 tablespoons chopped green onion
1 tablespoon butter
4 teaspoons cornstarch
1 cup orange juice
1 teaspoon instant chicken bouillon granules
1/2 teaspoon salt
1 orange, peeled, sectioned & diced

Secret
Ingredient:
Oranges

Arrange fish in a greased baking dish. In a small saucepan, cook onion and garlic in butter until tender. Stir cornstarch, bouillon and salt into orange juice. Add mixture to saucepan. Cook and stir until thickened. Stir in orange pieces and pour over fish. Bake at 350° for 17 to 20 minutes or until fish flakes easily with a fork.

The Secret Ingredient:

Side Dishes

Sweet Potato Casserole

6 sweet potatoes (about 4 pounds)
1/2 cup butter or margarine, melted
1/2 cup half & half
1/2 cup brown sugar, firmly packed
1/2 teaspoon salt
3 large eggs
1 teaspoon vanilla extract

Secret
Ingredient:
Gingersnap
Cookies

Cook sweet potatoes until tender. Cool, peel and mash. Add next 6 ingredients. Beat until smooth and spoon into a greased 2-1/2 quart shallow baking dish.

Crumb Topping:
1/4 cup butter, cut into small pieces
1/2 cup brown sugar, firmly packed
2 tablespoons all-purpose flour
16 coarsely crumbled gingersnap cookies
1/2 cup chopped pecans

In a medium bowl, combine brown sugar and flour. Cut in butter until crumbly. Stir in gingersnaps and pecans. Sprinkle topping over potato mixture. Bake at 350° for 25-30 minutes or until topping is lightly browned.

Rice Pilaf

2 tablespoons vegetable oil
1-1/4 cups uncooked long-grain rice
1 teaspoon dried basil (optional)
1 (10 oz.) can condensed French
    onion soup
1 (12 oz.) can of beer

Secret
Ingredient:
Beer

Heat oil in a saucepan over medium heat. Add rice and brown lightly, stirring constantly. Stir in basil, onion soup and beer. Cover and simmer for 20 minutes or until liquid is absorbed. Add salt and pepper to taste. Makes 6 servings.

Creamy Carrots

2-1/2 cups sliced carrots (about 3/4 lb.)
1/2 teaspoon cornstarch
1/2 cup whipping cream
2 tablespoons brown sugar, firmly packed
2 tablespoons chopped fresh mint leaves
1 tablespoon butter or margarine
1/2 teaspoon salt
1/4 teaspoon ground black pepper

Secret
Ingredient:
Mint

Cook carrots in boiling water 8-10 minutes or until tender; drain. In a small bowl, combine cornstarch and 2 teaspoons water; stir until smooth. In a small saucepan, bring cream to a boil. Stir in cornstarch mixture. Cook, stirring constantly, until thickened. Stir in remaining ingredients. Pour cream sauce over carrots and toss to coat.

Green Beans in Butter Sauce

1 pound fresh or frozen green beans
2 tablespoons butter
1 tablespoon dry white wine (optional)
1-1/2 teaspoons vanilla extract
1/2 teaspoon onion powder
1/4 teaspoon salt
1/8 teaspoon ground black pepper
1/4 cup sliced almonds, toasted*

Secret
Ingredient:
Vanilla
Extract

Cook beans, uncovered, in boiling water 5-6 minutes or until tender; drain. Melt butter in a small saucepan. Stir in wine, vanilla, onion powder, salt and pepper; simmer 2 minutes. Toss green beans with butter sauce. Top with toasted almonds.

*To toast almonds: Spread in single layer on baking sheet. Bake in 350° oven 3 – 5 minutes or until golden brown.

Dilled Green Peas

2 cups fresh green peas –OR–
   1 (10 oz.) package frozen peas
1 tablespoon butter or margarine
1/4 cup finely chopped onion
1 tablespoon chopped fresh dill
1/4 cup toasted walnuts*, chopped
Salt and pepper

Secret
Ingredient:
Walnuts

Cook peas in lightly salted, boiling water for 3-5 minutes or until tender; drain.

In a saucepan, melt butter. Add onion and sauté until tender. Stir in peas, dill and walnuts. Season with salt and pepper to taste.

*Toast walnuts in dry skillet over medium-high heat, stirring constantly for 3-5 minutes.

Texas Baked Beans

2 (15 ounce) cans pork and beans, drained
2 slices bacon
1/4 cup chopped onion
1/4 cup chopped green pepper
1/4 cup ketchup
1/4 cup brown sugar, packed
1/3 cup Dr. Pepper™
1 teaspoon prepared yellow mustard

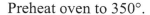

Secret
Ingredient:
Dr. Pepper

Preheat oven to 350°.

Cook bacon in a small skillet; remove, let cool and crumble. Cook onion and green pepper in bacon drippings until tender.

In a large bowl, combine beans, onion, green pepper, bacon, ketchup, sugar, mustard and Dr. Pepper. Pour into a greased casserole dish. Bake 40-45 minutes. Makes about 6-8 servings.

The
Secret
Ingredient:

Sandwiches

Chicken Salad Croissants

2 cups chopped cooked chicken
1/2 cup dried cherries, chopped
3 green onions, finely chopped
1/2 cup mayonnaise
1/4 cup sour cream
1 tablespoon lemon juice
Salt & ground black pepper to taste
Lettuce leaves
4 croissants

Secret
Ingredient:
Cherries

In a large bowl, combine chicken, cherries and onions. In a small bowl, combine mayonnaise, sour cream and lemon juice. Stir mayonnaise mixture into chicken mixture. Add salt and pepper to taste; blend well. Cover and refrigerate for several hours. Spoon chicken salad onto sliced croissants; top with lettuce.

Spicy Sloppy Joes

1-1/2 pounds ground sirloin
1/2 cup onion, chopped
1 cup cola beverage
1 cup barbecue sauce
6 hamburger buns

Secret
Ingredient:
Cola

In a large skillet, over medium-high heat, brown beef and onion until done. Reduce heat to medium; stir in cola and barbecue sauce. Bring to a boil and continue to cook, stirring occasionally, until sauce is thickened, about 10-15 minutes. Add salt and pepper to taste. Brush cut side of buns with melted butter and toast under broiler or in a skillet. Spoon meat mixture onto buns and serve.

Cheesy Pita Pockets

2-1/2 cups green or red
    seedless grapes
1/2 cup pecans, chopped
1/2 cup shredded cheddar cheese
1 (8 oz.) pkg. cream cheese, softened
2 tablespoons mayonnaise
1/2 teaspoon grated orange zest (optional)
1/4 teaspoon ground cinnamon
4 small pitas, halved
Lettuce (optional)

Secret
Ingredient:
Grapes

Blend together first 7 ingredients; mix well. Spread mixture inside pita pockets. Add lettuce if desired. Serves 4.

Pimiento Cheese Spread

2 cups shredded Cheddar cheese
1/4 cup chopped pimiento-stuffed
    green olives
1/3 cup mayonnaise
Salt & pepper to taste

Secret
Ingredient:
Olives

Combine all ingredients in a medium bowl; blend well. Cover and refrigerate until ready to serve. Use for sandwich filling with your favorite bread. Makes about four sandwiches.

Tangy Grilled Burgers

Secret
Ingredient:
Beer

Burgers:
1 large egg, slightly beaten
1/2 cup cracker crumbs
1/4 cup beer
1/4 cup finely chopped onion
1 tablespoon creamy French salad
    dressing
1 tablespoon grated parmesan cheese
1/4 teaspoon salt
1 lb. ground sirloin

Basting Sauce:
1/4 cup beer
1/4 cup creamy French salad dressing

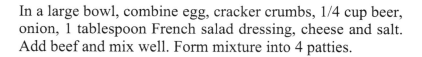

In a large bowl, combine egg, cracker crumbs, 1/4 cup beer, onion, 1 tablespoon French salad dressing, cheese and salt. Add beef and mix well. Form mixture into 4 patties.

For basting sauce, combine 1/4 cup beer and 1/4 cup French dressing in a small bowl.

Brush tops of burgers with sauce. Cook on grill or broil on a rack in the oven until done. Baste with sauce during cooking.

Hot Turkey Sandwiches

Honey Mustard Sauce:

1/2 cup mayonnaise
1 tablespoon honey
1 teaspoon prepared mustard

Secret
Ingredient:
Apples

In a small bowl, blend together all ingredients. Cover and refrigerate until ready to use.

Sandwiches:

8 slices whole grain bread
1 large apple, unpeeled, cored and thinly sliced
8 oz. sliced cooked turkey
4 oz. sliced Swiss cheese

To prepare sandwiches, spread each bread slice with mustard sauce. Place 4 of the bread slices on a baking sheet and top with apple slices, turkey and cheese, divided evenly among bread slices. Broil until cheese is melted. Top with remaining bread slices. Serve warm.

Pulled Pork Sandwiches

1 (2-1/2 to 3 lb.) pork roast
1/2 teaspoon salt
1/2 teaspoon pepper
1 tablespoon vegetable oil
2 medium onions, sliced
1 cup root beer
2 tablespoons minced garlic

Secret
Ingredient:
Root Beer

For Sauce:
2 (12-oz.) cans root beer
1 cup chili sauce
1/4 teaspoon hot pepper sauce (or to taste)

For Sandwiches:
8 to 10 hamburger buns
Lettuce leaves (optional)
Tomato slices (optional)

Sprinkle meat with salt and pepper. In a large skillet brown roast on all sides in oil. Transfer meat to a 3-1/2 to 4-quart slow cooker. Add onions, 1 cup root beer and garlic. Cover; cook on LOW for 8 to 10 hours or on HIGH for 4 to 5 hours.

To prepare sauce: In a medium saucepan combine 2 cans of root beer and chili sauce. Bring to boiling; reduce heat. Simmer, uncovered, stirring occasionally, about 30 minutes or until mixture is reduced to 2 cups. Add hot pepper sauce, if desired.

Remove roast from cooker. With a slotted spoon, remove onions from juices and place on serving platter. Discard juices. Using two forks, shred meat. To serve, place meat and onions on buns and spoon sauce over meat. Top with lettuce and tomato if desired.

The
Secret
Ingredient:

Sauces,
Rubs &
Gravies

Smokey Barbecue Sauce

1 cup ketchup
1 cup cola beverage
1/4 cup Worcestershire sauce
1 teaspoon liquid smoke
3 tablespoons steak sauce
1 teaspoon onion flakes
1 teaspoon garlic flakes
1/2 teaspoon ground black pepper

Secret
Ingredient:
Cola

Combine all ingredients in a saucepan and bring to a boil over medium heat. Reduce heat and simmer 6 to 8 minutes. Use immediately or cover and store in the refrigerator.

Balsamic Barbecue Sauce

1 tablespoon olive oil
1 tablespoon minced garlic
3/4 cup ketchup
1/2 cup balsamic vinegar
1/3 cup honey
1/4 cup soy sauce
1/4 cup strong black coffee
Dash of salt and ground black pepper
1 tablespoon orange zest

Secret
Ingredient:
Coffee

Heat oil in a saucepan over medium-low heat. Add garlic and sauté until golden. Whisk in the ketchup, vinegar, honey, soy sauce, and coffee. Simmer for 5 minutes to blend flavors. Remove from the heat. Season with salt and pepper, to taste and stir in orange zest. Recipe makes about 2 cups of sauce. Great on chicken or pork.

Polynesian Salsa

1/2 cup cucumber, peeled and diced
1/2 cup pineapple, diced
1/2 cup mango, peeled and diced
1/3 cup red bell pepper; diced
1/3 cup tomato, diced
3 tablespoons green onion, finely
    chopped

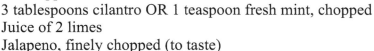

Secret
Ingredients:
Cucumber
& Mango

3 tablespoons cilantro OR 1 teaspoon fresh mint, chopped
Juice of 2 limes
Jalapeno, finely chopped (to taste)
Salt to taste

Blend all ingredients together in a small bowl. Cover and chill several hours to blend flavors. Serve with baked or grilled fish.

Sweet & Spicy Dry Rub

1 tablespoon brown sugar, packed
2 teaspoons onion powder
1-1/2 teaspoons unsweetened
    cocoa powder
1 teaspoon garlic powder
1/2 teaspoon chili powder
1/4 teaspoon ground paprika
1/4 teaspoon ground cinnamon

Secret
Ingredient:
Chocolate

In a small bowl, combine ingredients until well blended. Store in an airtight container. To use, sprinkle salt and pepper on pork chops, steaks or chicken. Rub spice mixture onto both sides of meat. Cover and refrigerate for at least one hour. Cook meat on grill until done.

New England Gravy

2 tablespoons butter or margarine
1/2 cup chopped onion
2 tablespoons all-purpose flour
1/4 teaspoon seasoned salt
1/8 teaspoon garlic powder
1 cup chicken broth
1/4 cup maple syrup or pancake syrup
1 tablespoon Dijon mustard

Secret Ingredient: Maple Syrup

In a large saucepan, melt butter and sauté onion until tender. Stir in flour, seasoned salt and garlic powder. Cook stirring for 1 minute. Stir in broth and cook until thickened. Stir in remaining ingredients. Bring to a boil and simmer 2 minutes or until thickened.

Thanksgiving Day Gravy

1 (10-1/2 oz.) can condensed chicken broth
2 tablespoons lemon juice
1 (16 oz.) can jellied cranberry sauce
  (or whole cranberry sauce)
1-1/2 tablespoons cornstarch
Salt and pepper to taste

Secret Ingredient: Cranberry Sauce

In a large saucepan, combine chicken broth and lemon juice. Cook over medium heat until boiling. Add cranberry sauce, stirring until dissolved and thoroughly heated through. In a small cup, blend cornstarch with 2 tablespoons water. Stir into gravy and cook until slightly thickened. Add salt and pepper to taste. Serve with turkey and dressing.

The
Secret
Ingredient:

Desserts

Chocolate Snack Cake

2 cups all-purpose flour
1 cup granulated sugar
1-1/2 teaspoons baking soda
1/3 cup unsweetened cocoa powder
1/4 teaspoon salt
1 cup coffee, room temperature
1 cup real mayonnaise
1 teaspoon vanilla extract
1/2 cup semi-sweet chocolate chips
1/4 cup chopped walnuts or pecans

Secret
Ingredients:
Mayonnaise
& Coffee

Preheat oven to 350°. In a large bowl, blend first 5 ingredients together. In a separate bowl, whisk together coffee, mayonnaise and vanilla. Add flour mixture to mayonnaise mixture; blend well. Stir in chocolate chips and nuts. Pour batter into a greased and floured 9" square pan. Bake for 30-35 minutes or until done. Cool in pan and cut into squares to serve. Top with whipped cream if desired.

Hurry-Up Cherry Cobbler

2 (21 oz.) cans cherry pie filling
1 (18 oz.) package yellow cake mix
1 (12 oz.) can 7-Up

Secret
Ingredient:
7-Up

Preheat oven to 350°.

Pour pie filling into a 9" X 13" baking dish. Sprinkle dry cake mix over pie filling. Pour 7-Up over cake mix. Bake for 45 minutes. Serve warm or cold with sweetened whipped cream or ice cream.

Crock Pot Spice Cake

1 (10-3/4 oz.) can condensed
    tomato soup
1/2 cup water
2 large eggs
1 box (about 18 oz.) spice cake mix
1-1/4 cups hot water
3/4 cup brown sugar, firmly packed
1 teaspoon ground cinnamon
Vanilla ice cream or sweetened whipped cream

Secret
Ingredient:
Tomato
Soup

Lightly grease the inside of a 3-1/2 to 4 quart crock pot. In a large bowl, mix soup, 1/2 cup water, eggs and cake mix. Pour into crock pot. In a small bowl, mix 1-1/4 cups hot water, brown sugar and cinnamon. Pour over batter. Do not stir. Cover and cook on high 2 to 2-1/2 hours or until toothpick inserted in center comes out clean. To serve, spoon warm cake into bowls, scooping sauce from bottom of crock pot. Serve cake warm with ice cream or whipped cream on top.

Creamy Chocolate Fudge

1 cup (2 sticks) butter or margarine
8 oz. Velveeta cheese
1/2 cup unsweetened cocoa powder
1 teaspoon vanilla extract
2 lb. powdered sugar
1 cup chopped pecans

Secret
Ingredient:
Velveeta
Cheese

Slowly melt butter and cheese over low heat, or in a microwave, stirring frequently until smooth. Add cocoa and vanilla; mix well. Stir in powdered sugar and nuts. Press into a buttered 9" X 13" pan. Chill and cut into squares. Store fudge in an air tight container in the refrigerator.

Chocolate Chip Crunchies

1/2 cup brown sugar, packed
1/2 cup granulated sugar
1/2 cup butter, softened
1 large egg
1/2 teaspoon vanilla extract
1 cup all-purpose flour
1/2 teaspoon baking soda
1 cup crushed potato chips   1/4 cup chopped nuts
1/2 cup semi-sweet chocolate chips

Secret Ingredient: Potato Chips

Preheat oven to 350°. In a large bowl, cream together sugars, butter, eggs and vanilla. In a separate bowl, blend flour, baking soda, potato chips, chocolate chips and nuts. Stir into sugar mixture. Drop by teaspoonfuls onto lightly greased cookie sheet. Bake for 8 - 10 minutes or until done. Remove to wire racks to cool.

Chocolate Toffee Cake

1 (4 serving size) box instant
    chocolate pudding
2 cups milk
10 Hostess® Twinkie singles
1 cup (8 oz.) toffee bits
1 (8 oz.) container frozen non-dairy
    whipped topping, thawed

Secret Ingredient: Twinkies

Prepare pudding with milk as directed on package. Set aside. Slice Twinkies in half lengthwise. Line the bottom of a 13" x 9" baking dish with the Twinkie halves, filling side up. Sprinkle 1/2 cup toffee bits over Twinkies. Pour pudding on top. Spread whipped topping over pudding. Top with remaining toffee bits. Cover and refrigerate until ready to serve.

Sugar Plum Cake

2 cups granulated sugar
1 cup vegetable oil
3 large eggs
1 (4 oz.) jar of plum baby food
1 (4 oz.) jar of apricot baby food
2 cups self-rising flour
1 teaspoon ground cinnamon
1/4 teaspoon ground cloves
1 cup chopped pecans or walnuts

Secret
Ingredient:
Baby
Food

Preheat oven to 350°. Grease and flour a 10" tube pan.

In a large bowl, beat together sugar, oil, eggs and baby food. Add flour and spices; blend well. Stir in nuts. Pour batter into prepared pan and bake for 50-55 minutes or until done. Remove from pan and place on a wire rack to cool. Frost with Cream Cheese Frosting if desired.

Cream Cheese Frosting

1 (8 oz.) package cream cheese, softened
1/2 stick butter or margarine, softened
1 teaspoon vanilla extract
1/2 (1lb. box) of powdered sugar

Beat cream cheese, butter and vanilla together until well blended. Gradually add powdered sugar until desired consistency.

Frosted Chocolate Brownies

1 cup (2 sticks) butter
3 tablespoons unsweetened cocoa powder
1 cup cola beverage
2 cups all-purpose flour
2 cups granulated sugar
1/4 teaspoon salt
1 teaspoon baking soda
1/2 cup buttermilk
2 large eggs, slightly beaten
1 teaspoon vanilla extract

Secret
Ingredient:
Cola

Frosting:
6 tablespoons cola beverage
3 tablespoons unsweetened cocoa powder
1/2 cup (1 stick) butter
1 (1 lb.) box powdered sugar
1 cup finely chopped walnuts (optional)
1 teaspoon vanilla extract

To Prepare Cake: Preheat oven to 350°. In a large bowl, blend together flour, sugar and salt. In a saucepan, heat butter, cocoa and cola until mixture comes to a boil. Remove from heat and stir into flour mixture. In a small bowl blend together buttermilk, eggs, baking soda and vanilla. Stir into flour mixture. Pour into greased 9"x13" pan. Bake 30 to 35 minutes or until done. Frost brownies while warm.

To Prepare Icing: In a large saucepan, heat butter, cocoa, and cola until boiling. Remove from heat and stir in powdered sugar, nuts and vanilla. Spread on top of warm brownies.

Rosy Apple Pie

6 cups sliced, peeled cooking apples
1/3 cup ketchup
2 teaspoons lemon juice
1 unbaked, 9" pie shell

Secret
Ingredient:
Ketchup

Crumb Topping:
2/3 cup flour
1/3 cup sugar
1 teaspoon cinnamon
1/3 cup butter, chilled

To Prepare the Pie:
Preheat oven to 425°. In a large bowl, mix together ketchup and lemon juice. (Add 2 tablespoons of granulated sugar to this mixture if apples are very tart.) Stir in apples. Pour into pie shell.

To Prepare the Topping:
Combine flour, sugar and cinnamon. Cut in butter until mixture resembles coarse crumbs. Sprinkle over apples. Bake 40-45 minutes. Cool completely before serving.

Ranchero Pie

1/2 cup granulated sugar
1 cup brown sugar, firmly packed
1/2 cup butter or margarine
2 large eggs
1 heaping cup mashed, cooked pinto
    beans (canned is fine)
1 unbaked 9" pie shell
Whipped topping (optional)

Secret
Ingredient:
Pinto
Beans

Preheat oven to 375°. In a large bowl, cream together sugars and butter. Beat in eggs. Stir in beans; blend well. Pour into unbaked pie shell and bake for 20 minutes. Reduce heat to 350° and bake an additional 25 minutes or until knife inserted in center comes out clean. Serve with whipped topping if desired.

Cool & Creamy Chocolate Torte

16 flour tortillas
4 cups sour cream
1 (16 oz.) pkg. semi-sweet
    chocolate chips
1 teaspoon almond extract
1 (16 oz.) container frozen
    non-dairy whipped topping, thawed

Secret
Ingredient:
Tortillas

Place chocolate chips in a large microwaveable bowl. Microwave on HIGH power, stirring after each 30 seconds until melted and smooth. Add sour cream and almond extract and mix well. Place one tortilla on a plate and spread with about 1/4 cup chocolate mixture. Top with another tortilla and repeat for remaining tortillas. Frost stack of tortillas with whipped topping. Cover and refrigerate until ready to serve. Slice into wedges to serve.

Luscious Lemon-Lime Pie

1-1/4 cups crushed pretzels
1/4 cup granulated sugar
6 tablespoons butter or
   margarine, melted
1 (14 oz.) can sweetened
   condensed milk
1/2 cup lime juice
1 envelope Kool-Aid Lemon Lime
   Unsweetened Soft Drink Mix
1 (8 oz.) container non-dairy frozen whipped topping,
   thawed & divided

Secret
Ingredient:
Kool-Aid

In a small bowl, mix together crushed pretzels, sugar and butter. Press firmly onto bottom and up sides of 9" pie plate. Refrigerate until ready to fill.

In a large bowl, combine condensed milk, lime juice and drink mix until well blended. Remove 1/2 cup whipped topping from container and set aside. Gently stir in remaining 2-1/2 cups of whipped topping. Pour into prepared crust.

Cover and freeze pie several hours until firm. Let stand at room temperature 15 minutes before cutting. To serve, top each slice with dollop of reserved whipped topping. Store leftover pie in freezer.

Golden Glazed Bundt Cake

Cake:
1 (18 oz.) package white cake mix
1 (12 oz.) can root beer
1/4 cup vegetable oil
3 large eggs

Secret Ingredient: Root Beer

Glaze:
1/2 cup powdered sugar
3 tablespoons root beer

Preheat oven to 350°. Grease and flour a 10" Bundt pan. In a large bowl, combine cake mix, root beer, oil and eggs. Blend until smooth. Pour into prepared pan. Bake 35-40 minutes or until toothpick inserted in center comes out clean. Cool 15 minutes in pan. Turn out onto wire rack to cool. To prepare the glaze, mix powdered sugar with 3 tablespoons of root beer until smooth. Poke holes in cake using a skewer or wooden pick and pour glaze over top.

Chocolate Coconut Candy

1 (1 lb.) box powdered sugar
8 oz. sweetened, shredded coconut
2/3 cup mashed, cooked potato
1/2 teaspoon vanilla extract
1 cup semi-sweet chocolate chips
2 tablespoons milk

Secret Ingredient: Mashed Potatoes

Combine sugar, coconut, potato and vanilla until smooth. Spread in bottom of a buttered 9" square baking dish. Place chocolate chips and milk in a small, microwaveable bowl. Cook on MEDIUM power until melted and smooth, stirring at 30 second intervals. Spread on top of potato mixture. Cover and chill 2 hours. Cut into squares.

Mock Apple Pie

Secret Ingredient: Crackers

2 cups granulated sugar
1-3/4 cups water
1/2 teaspoon ground cinnamon
2 teaspoons cream of tartar
2 tablespoons lemon juice
1 teaspoon grated lemon zest
36 buttery crackers, coarsely broken (about 1-3/4 cups)
1 (15 oz.) package of refrigerated pastry dough
    (2 pie crusts for 9" pie)
2 tablespoons of butter or margarine

In a large sauce pan, blend sugar, water, cinnamon and cream of tartar. Bring to a boil. Reduce heat and simmer 15 minutes. Add lemon juice. Set aside to cool.

Preheat oven to 425°. Unroll one pastry and fit inside bottom of pie pan.

Place crackers in bottom of prepared pie crust. Dot with pieces of the butter. Pour sugar mixture over crackers. Cover with top crust. Crimp edges and cut several slits in the top with a knife for vents. Bake about 30 minutes or until top crust is golden brown. Cool completely before serving.

Index

Crunchy Pinto Bean Salad, 27
Garden Tuna Salad, 26
Pork Tenderloin Salad, 28

Sandwiches:
Chicken Salad Croissants, 48
Cheesy Pita Pockets, 49
Hot Turkey Sandwiches, 51
Pimiento Cheese Spread, 49
Pulled Pork Sandwiches, 52
Spicy Sloppy Joes, 48
Tangy Grilled Burgers, 50

Sauces, Rubs & Gravies:
Balsamic Barbecue Sauce, 54
New England Gravy, 56
Polynesian Salsa, 55
Smokey Barbecue Sauce, 54
Sweet & Spicy Dry Rub, 55
Thanksgiving Day Gravy, 56

Side Dishes:
Creamy Carrots, 43
Dilled Green Peas, 45
Green Beans in Butter Sauce, 44
Rice Pilaf, 43
Sweet Potato Casserole, 42
Texas Baked Beans, 46

Soups & Stews:
Autumn Harvest Beef Stew, 34
Chilled Honeydew Soup, 32
Georgia Planter's Soup, 30
Greek Chicken Soup, 31
Ranch Hand Beef Soup, 33
Real Man's Chili, 32
Santa Fe Tortilla Soup, 33
Southern Belle Blush, 30

About the Author

Gloria Hander Lyons has channeled 30 years of training and hands-on experience in the areas of art, interior decorating, crafting and event planning into writing creative how-to books. Her books cover a wide range of topics including decorating your home, cooking, planning weddings and tea parties, crafting and self-publishing.

She has designed original craft projects featured in magazines, such as *Better Homes and Gardens, McCall's, Country Handcrafts* and *Crafts*.

She teaches interior decorating, self-publishing and wedding planning classes at her local community college, as well as private classes and workshops. Much to her family's delight, her kitchen is in non-stop test mode, creating recipes for new cookbooks.

Visit her website for free craft ideas, decorating and event planning tips and recipes at: www.BlueSagePress.com.

Other Books by Gloria Hander Lyons

- *Easy Microwave Desserts in a Mug*
- *Easy Microwave Desserts in a Mug for Kids*
- *No Rules – Just Fun Decorating*
- *Just Fun Decorating for Tweens & Teens*
- *Decorating Basics: For Men Only!*
- *If Teapots Could Talk—Fun Ideas for Tea Parties*
- *Teapots & Teddy Bears—Fun Ideas for Children's Tea Parties*
- *The Super-Bride's Guide for Dodging Wedding Pitfalls*
- *Designs That Sell: How To Make Your Home Show Better and Sell Faster*
- *A Taste of Lavender: Delectable Treats with an Exotic Floral Flavor*
- *Lavender Sensations: Fragrant Herbs for Home & Bath*
- *Self-Publishing on a Budget: A Do-It-All-Yourself Guide*
- *Hand Over the Chocolate & No One Gets Hurt! A Chocolate-Lover's Cookbook*
- *Flamingoes, Poodle Skirts & Red Hots: Creative Theme Party Ideas*

Ordering Information

To order additional copies of this book, send check or money order payable to:

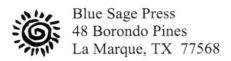 Blue Sage Press
48 Borondo Pines
La Marque, TX 77568

Cost for this edition is $7.95 per book (U.S. currency only) plus $3.50 shipping and handling for the first book and $1.50 for each additional book shipped to the same U.S. address.

Texas residents add 8.25% sales tax to total order amount.

To pay by credit card or get a complete list of books written by Gloria Hander Lyons, visit our website at:

www.BlueSagePress.com.

2555699R00040

Printed in Great Britain
by Amazon.co.uk, Ltd.,
Marston Gate.